O9-AID-639

99

THOUGHTs
for small group
leaders

tips for
rookies & veterans
on leading youth ministry
small groups

Joshua Griffin
with Doug Fields

99 Thoughts for Small Group Leaders
Youth Ministry Tips for Leading Your Small Group

Copyright © 2010 Simply Youth Ministry

group.com
simplyyouthministry.com

Credits
Authors: Joshua Griffin with Doug Fields
Executive Developer: Nadim Najm
Chief Creative Officer: Joani Schultz
Editor: Matt McGill
Copy Editor: Rob Cunningham
Cover Art and Production: Riley Hall & Veronica Lucas
Production Manager: DeAnne Lear
Back Cover Photo Credit: www.alannamoine.com

ISBN 978-0-7644-4680-1

10 9 8 7 6 5 4 3   18 17 16 15 14 13 12 11 10

Printed in the United States of America.

DEDICATION

To the best small group leaders
in the world: my mom and dad,
Bob and Teresa Griffin.

- Josh

To those who sacrifice most
for what I'm called to do...
Cathy, Torie, Cody, and Cassie

-Doug

TABLE OF CONTENTS

**** We realize this book has more than 99 thoughts in it and it's mostly because we didn't know when to stop... and we didn't want to change the title of the book. So, treat it like that little surprise you get when you discover a $5 bill in your pocket. ****

I have been in youth ministry for almost 20 years and I have never written a foreword for a book before. I am assuming I have never been asked because I am not that famous—nor do I consider myself an expert in this field. However, I am a youth worker who **LOVES** and **BELIEVES** in small group ministry. So, the opportunity to be a part of this book in some small way was really hard for me to pass up. There are two reasons I am ridiculously excited about the pages you are about to read: Reason one, I adore Josh Griffin and Doug Fields and their heart for small group leaders, and reason two, I am a small group leader and always want to learn more.

Over the years, small groups have become my very favorite area of youth ministry. I have led 14 small groups in my youth ministry career, and I have come to realize that there is something so special about being a small group leader of teenagers. I love showing up each week to see "my" girls and to minister to them in a way that no one else does. Small group leading has been a source of total joy and has filled my ministry years with incredible memories.

That is why I am so excited for small group leaders to possess this book. Even though leading small groups has been awesome, it has not been without challenges. Between preparing a relevant lesson, dealing with the emotional needs of my students, and trying to be fun and creative, I often find myself looking in various places for inspiration and ideas. That is where this book comes in.

This book is a great resource for all small group leaders to gain insight, gather ideas, and even stretch ourselves beyond what we think we can do in the lives of teenagers. As you work through the pages of this book, I encourage you to mark up the margins, make these ideas your own, and challenge yourself to try something new in your small group ministry.

I have watched Josh and Doug pour their heart and soul into small group leaders week after week, and I am excited for you to get a taste of what our leaders get.

Katie

Katie Edwards
Junior High Minister, Saddleback Church

INTRODUCTION

Small groups are the backbone of our youth ministry.

Sure, other programs may be more visible, so the casual observer would think that those might be the most important within a youth ministry. We love worship services and special events because they are the smiling face of our youth ministry. But, if small groups were a body part, they would be the vital backbone. They are central to the health of youth ministry life. Without small groups, our ministry would just be a show.

At times, small groups can be a total pain. I've* had to sandpaper off the screwdriver marks left by a student carving his name into a coffee table in a host home. I've had to pay for broken couches out of an already dwindling youth budget. I've had to organize students into groups a hundred times before getting it right—only to completely change it a week later.

But as much as small groups are challenging to organize, they are totally worth it. I've seen lives completely changed—one minute a teenager is walking away from God, and the next minute they're embracing Jesus as Savior. I've seen students dive deeper into their faith and hold onto each other in vibrant spiritual community.

And that kind of stuff seems to make resurfacing coffee tables and couch repair pretty insignificant.

The face of youth ministry will change over time, but good youth ministry will always include a team of caring adults pouring their lives into teenagers. Whoever put this book into your hands believes in you and believes you are going to make a difference in the lives of teenagers and wants to equip you for the journey. I know you can do it!

Blessings to you on that journey!

Joshua Griffin
Youth Ministry Team, Saddleback Church
morethandodgeball.com

* **SPECIAL NOTE:** I wrote this book alongside my good friend and mentor, Doug Fields. As we were writing, it became obnoxious to try to explain whose voice owned a feeling or an illustration. So, instead of writing, "I (Josh) love Star Wars" and "I (Doug) enjoy mountain biking," we ditched our names and assumed you wouldn't care and would rather have an easier read.

140 Throughout the book you'll find boxes just like this. These are 140-character, Twitter™-sized summaries or commentary on the thoughts. Use them as helps or tips that you can reference as you work with your small group.

Thoughts **1-29**

WHERE TO
STARt

So you signed on to be a small group leader. Awesome! Here's some quick ideas to get you started in your new role.

WHO WE ARE CALLED TO MINISTER TO

Thanks for committing to serve as a small group leader! Your faithful service will not go unnoticed. So what exactly are we dealing with here when we're called, asked, or begged to be a small group leader of a teenager? Good question!

Here is a simple profile of a typical teenager:

He/she is quickly adopting the lifestyle of their parents—fast and furious. In our student ministry we recently asked students what the number one issue was in their lives; they answered, "Dealing with stress." Chances are good that this answer wouldn't have been the same 10 years ago.

With an already packed schedule, students are confronted with college earlier than ever before— the competition is fierce. On the morality front, not a minute passes without them being bombarded with twisted messages of sexuality from reality shows or musical acts, driving them to repetitively defend their values until, unfortunately, the time comes when many give up and give in.

On the technological front, typical students live and die by their cell phones—their thumbs can text faster than you can probably type. They can get movie times, find the nearest Starbucks®, and have access to pornography quicker than any time in history. Social networking is important—they're online several times throughout the day. With the emergence of smart phones, being tethered to social media has gone from fad to epidemic. Recovery groups have formed to help deal with the resulting addiction.

Another area competing to influence them are the many different worldviews that are out there. Their worldview is being shaped by people who advocate tolerance but shut down most expressions of faith. Teenagers are very interested in being spiritual but not necessarily being Christians. They are searching frantically for acceptance and consistency. They are growing up in a culture that encourages them to be politically correct at the expense of taking a stand for their faith. The war is raging, and they are as confused as a child faced with the question of whether they want to live with mom or dad after the divorce.

And that's where YOU come in!

If you are young... things aren't much different than when you were in school, but be careful not to be overconfident in your ability to relate to teenagers, because a lot *has* changed!

If you are older (over 30 is old to a teenager) ... things might feel very different from when you were a teenager and you might be intimidated or feel out of touch. That's normal, and actually, I prefer to have adults who are a little afraid—it reveals humility and dependance. These are good, healthy responses and will ready you to lead well.

Here's what hasn't changed: No matter what your age is, teenagers still need love, acceptance, and care. They deeply desire to be known and desperately need to be wisely and lovingly guided to Jesus.

So hear this: You are a conduit of hope. You are the leader. Who will guide teenagers to sorting through the mess they're confronting? With God's Spirit working through you, you can do it. You can do it well!

THE 6 ROLES OF A SMALL GROUP LEADER

What you are doing is a big deal—you will have to wear many different hats. Here are a few of the ones you will need to wear:

You are...

1. A spiritual leader

Your students are listening to your faith and watching your life. They are counting on you having a genuine (not perfect) walk with Jesus. Always know that your faith is lived out loud by your actions and not just your words. Even when you slip up, you show spiritual leadership in the way you humbly and correctly deal with mistakes and strive for God's best.

2. A youth pastor/shepherd

Your students are counting on you to notice when they're gone. They expect you to call them out (in love) when they miss the mark on God's standards and their intended commitments. They are waiting for that personal challenge. You are essentially a pastor in this small group movement that God has been using to develop Christ-followers since the early church. You get to lead students into this deep-level relational and spiritual journey. Some days this will be seen as a wild stroke of good fortune; other days it will be an inescapable weighty albatross of death.

3. **Part of the youth ministry team**
Your leadership can greatly help or cause crippling hurt to the student ministry of your church. Be a team player and remember that you are part of the whole. Your small group isn't a separate youth group, it's just one part of the overall strategy within a youth ministry.

4. **An administrative wizard**
Just kidding. Just wanted to see if you're still paying attention. Although it wouldn't hurt if you could remember where your Bible is, how to send an e-mail or text, and what time your group meets. Leave all the administrative details to the person in charge.

5. **A teacher**
Your students are counting on you to open God's Word and help them learn how to discover and live by God's plan. You don't need to have a doctorate in theology, be a stand-up comic, or have a

Shakespearian stage presence. Your heart for God and your relationship with him will shine through your teaching.

For it to shine through, you've got to have the light shining brightly within you. More on that later.

6. A relational guide

The small group is all about community. You are the facilitator of those connections and relationships. Students come to group carrying a variety of emotional baggage (dejection, rejection, insecurity) and high on life (life happened to go well that day, closeness with God, eager to grow in their faith). Caring for a group of students who bring such a wide variety of circumstances with them will require your flexibility, sensitivity, and wisdom. After all, how do we rejoice with those who rejoice and mourn with those who mourn simultaneously? Experience will bring the answer.

Hang in there!

Students are listening with their ears and watching with their eyes. Small group leaders teach and model God's ways.

Live a life filled with love, following the example of Christ. He loved us and offered himself as a sacrifice for us, a pleasing aroma to God.

(Ephesians 5:2)

4 WAYS SMALL GROUP LEADERS ARE SPIRITUAL LEADERS

Let's focus a little more closely on one of the six primary functions of volunteer leaders from the previous pages. Here's a little more on what I believe is the first and most important role of all: a spiritual leader.

7. They walk with God: Genuine faith and committed to walk with Jesus.

Effective small group leaders spend time with God, pray, and model spiritual disciplines. They give plenty of grace for the ups and downs of walking with Christ, but overall there's an expectation that leaders are growing on their own. This isn't a requirement for perfection. Most importantly, I want small group leaders to have hearts that are sensitive to God's leading and Spirit.

8. They model community: Pursuing healthy friendships and relationships.

Just like we challenge students to join a small group to experience community, it would make sense that we as adults would share this same value, too. I realize this is an additional commitment and possibly another night out of the week, but modeling community will not only increase your integrity, but also help you in your own walk with Jesus. Healthy small group leaders connect with other God-loving adults who sharpen them. A leader who teaches without being renewed will burn out, shrivel spiritually, or puff up with pride—all poor scenarios.

9. They are accountable: Genuinely pursuing accountability in your life.

The small group leader should seek to have healthy accountability in his or her life—and a teenage small group is not the place for all your accountability and confession. I'm not suggesting you never share vulnerably with teenagers (of course you should), but you should have other outlets for your personal accountability.

10. They participate in worship: Attend a church service regularly.

Church attendance is also important in the life of a small group leader. We are part of our church and want to be connected to the overall vision and direction of our senior pastor. As a small group leader, you will be pouring out and emptying yourself, so it's wise to be continually filled up as well—a church worship service definitely plays a role in being full.

140

The primary role of a small group leader is to be a spiritual leader. It starts with you, your walk with God, and your connection to community.

Dear brothers and sisters, if another believer is overcome by some sin, you who are godly should gently and humbly help that person back onto the right path. And be careful not to fall into the same temptation yourself. Share each other's burdens, and in this way obey the law of Christ. If you think you are too important to help someone, you are only fooling yourself. You are not that important.

(Galatians 6:1-3)

Youth Ministry Heroes

I'm pretty confident that leading a small group is the toughest role a youth ministry volunteer can choose to play (hosting a sixth-grade lock-in would be a close second though). Think about it: When a volunteer agrees to be a small group leader, this person is agreeing to some sort of variation of the following:

- Becoming a pastor to a dozen high-maintenance teenagers.

- Preparing a lesson every week.

- Spending their own money with "broke" students at McDonald's, Pizza Hut, and Taco Bell.

- Financing their cholesterol medicine because of McDonald's, Pizza Hut, and Taco Bell.

- Taking phone calls from panicky parents at all hours of the night.

- Learning how to really listen and not just provide easy answers.

- Sacrificing time with their own family.

The list could really go on and on, but you get the point: Volunteer small group leaders are the unsung heroes of your church!

-Kurt

Kurt Johnston is the Pastor of Student Ministries at Saddleback Church and a seasoned youth worker who values the importance of volunteers.

6 REMINDERS
WHEN MINISTERING
TO STUDENTS

Refresh yourself with the Apostle Paul's words from 1 Thessalonians:

> **¹²Dear brothers and sisters,** *honor those who are your leaders in the Lord's work. They work hard among you and give you spiritual guidance. ¹³Show them great respect and wholehearted love because of their work. And live peacefully with each other.*

> *¹⁴Brothers and sisters, we urge you to warn those who are lazy. Encourage those who are timid. Take tender care of those who are weak. Be patient with everyone.*

> *¹⁵See that no one pays back evil for evil, but always try to do good to each other and to all people.*

> *¹⁶Always be joyful. ¹⁷Never stop praying. ¹⁸Be thankful in all circumstances, for this is God's will for you who belong to Christ Jesus.*

[19]Do not stifle the Holy Spirit. [20]Do not scoff at prophecies, [21]but test everything that is said. Hold on to what is good. [22]Stay away from every kind of evil.

[23]Now may the God of peace make you holy in every way, and may your whole spirit and soul and body be kept blameless until our Lord Jesus Christ comes again. [24]God will make this happen, for he who calls you is faithful.

[25]Dear brothers and sisters, pray for us.

[26]Greet all the brothers and sisters with Christian love.

[27]I command you in the name of the Lord to read this letter to all the brothers and sisters.

[28]May the grace of our Lord Jesus Christ be with you.

(1 Thessalonians 5:12-28)

The context of this passage represents the second coming of Christ and how followers of Jesus—awake or asleep—someday will be with him. Then Paul gives some specific actions to those who are alive.

In the context of youth ministry, here are some thoughts that I find appropriate to those of us who shepherd teenagers:

11. Help the weak (v. 14)

We share in the privilege of serving students who are hurting and lost. It is our honor to help those that are stumbling to walk again and those who are seeking to find God. What a sacred calling we share in our ministry to teenagers.

12. Be patient (v. 14)

Have you ever had "that one kid" in your small group? By last count, we felt like half of our student ministry was filled with "that one kid." If you don't now, you will probably have at least one in your group very soon. Paul leaves us with a key challenge to be patient, longsuffering, slow to anger, slow to punish, and quick to bear the offense of a teenager who speaks quickly and thinks later. Difficult to do? Yes! Impossible? No!

13. Pray continually (v. 17)

A powerful tool for small group leaders is our ability to go directly to God as we minister. Share your insecurities and your inadequacies, and God will fill you with his Spirit to give you the words to say and actions to take. When in doubt, pray.

14. **Be thankful God is using you (v. 18)**
God has put you in your small group for this moment! He calls and enables you to work with the specific students in your group. If a crisis happens, you are uniquely, relationally, and spiritually positioned to help teenagers through dark moments. Seek to be continually thankful for the honor of serving God as a small group leader.

15. **Remember that God is faithful (v. 24)**
God will use his Word and your words to minister to students. You might not always "feel" God working through you, and your words might not always seem usable by God, but God is faithful! The pressure is on God to fulfill his promise that his Word won't return void... the pressure is on you to be fruitful.

16. **Know the team is behind you (v. 25)**
Don't serve alone! Rely on others from your youth ministry team and church for support and wisdom as you serve and care for students. As the shepherds of teenagers, we do well to support

each other, keep each other accountable, and share life (and many meals) together. We are better together!

140

You are making a difference in students' lives. You will hear that again in heaven some day.

4 REASONS
WHY WE HAVE
SMALL GROUPS

So why do I believe in small groups so much? Because the lower the adult to teenager ratio, the more intentional discipleship appears. Here are four "whys" of small groups:

17. Care: Small groups make a large crowd (over six) feel small.

Kids can hide in larger groups but they can't hide in small groups! The anonymity a larger group offers can be great, but the attention to individuals in a small group is usually where lives are changed. Instead of being an unknown in a crowd, small groups help students be known and loved as individuals.

18. Growth: Small groups are an integral part of a discipleship process.

A small group is a gateway to encouraging teenagers to serve and grow deeper in their faith.

A breakdown here can hinder the next steps of spiritual growth, weaken a commitment to serve in ministry, or suppress a passion for evangelism.

19. Wisdom: This is the result of the power that appears when an adult life intersects with a teenage life.

A leader like you, who has traveled down the path of life a little further, can provide insight, life-altering encouragement, and wisdom-laden warnings for students.

20. Accountability: Positive peer pressure and reinforcement.

Being in a small group with other committed Christians encourages students to become accountable to each other and provides a format for teenagers to speak truth into each other's lives. Imagine a group where students encourage one another on God's path; where Christ-like wisdom is sought and shared; a place where poor choices are addressed with love and a boundary set in place to guide wayward students. Ideally, small groups provide this type of environment where attention and motivation appear.

Other whys of small groups: inside jokes, late-night runs to Denny's, belly laughs, road trips, and 3D movies.

Let us hold tightly without wavering to the hope we affirm, for God can be trusted to keep his promise. Let us think of ways to motivate one another to acts of love and good works. And let us not neglect our meeting together, as some people do, but encourage one another, especially now that the day of his return is drawing near.

(Hebrews 10:23-25)

WHAT IS RELATIONAL MINISTRY?

Relational youth ministry happens when you take any step toward building a friendship with a student in your small group. It could be a big or small step—either way, it is an effort toward entering into a relational community and sharing life together.

I want our youth ministry to be known for genuine relationships! I want our students known, loved, and cared for. It all takes time—and one of the entries into a teenager's life is to enter into their world in a tangible way. This can happen through some simple starting options. When you go to a student's sporting event, that's an example of an amazing start toward relational ministry. You couldn't make it to the game, but sent a text asking if they won or not? Still, that's a great move toward developing and deepening a relationship. You thought about them or prayed for them while they played? I'll take it! I spoke with a leader recently who told me about simple ways he connects with students—from road trips to campouts, from birthday parties to a "good luck on the SAT" text. All efforts make a difference and help toward building relationships.

Too often, small group leaders think the key relational steps require a lot of time. Well, some weeks they may, and some weeks, small steps are huge. As a small group leader, just commit to taking some steps to be relational and build community with the students God has entrusted to you!

Most important of all, continue to show deep love for each other, for love covers a multitude of sins. Cheerfully share your home with those who need a meal or a place to stay.

(1 Peter 4:8-9)

A focus on relational youth ministry gives...

21. ...students an increased ownership of ministry/faith

Students who have a significant relationship with a caring adult tend to stick; it's as simple as that. Students don't fall through the cracks when they are known, loved, and cared for. Sure, some students will still wander away. It's possible that even an extreme effort won't save some teenagers from leaving the church and/or Christian community. However, as a general rule, when adults invest in students, those who "stick" will develop a healthy ownership of both their faith and serving in a ministry.

22. ...leaders a more holistic picture of students' lives

If you minister to a student for the two hours a week of official small group time, that's good enough. But what if you could add a "+" to those two hours (even a small "+")?

The "+" could be simple—a text, a call, a Twitter™ update with their name in it, or a message through Facebook™. Even little efforts net big results with teenagers.

The "+" could also require something that's not so simple—a visit to a student's volleyball game, a visit to the home, showing up at a school play, and so on (basically, any presence requires time, and time is a big sacrifice). Whatever the effort may be, it will give you a better glimpse into the world of teenagers. You'll better understand them and how to effectively minister to their needs.

23. ...everyone more openness to share

When there are relationships in a small group, lives open up for deep and vulnerable discussions. Discussions go beyond the usual, superficial and safe chatter. There are nights when groups clam up—it happens, so don't lose sleep over it! But as a general rule, if you want your group to share, then become invested in their lives.

[See page 69 for more about becoming invested in students' lives.]

3 MESSAGES
OF RELATIONAL
MINISTRY

Relational small group leaders breathe life into their students when they communicate:

24. "I care"

Simply put, when you make a step to connect with a student, your actions scream how much you care. In a teenage world of too-busy parents, virtual friendships, and fast-paced relationships, your efforts to develop a relationship with teenagers shows how deeply you care for them. Every minute you spend with them, every text you send, every time you show up—it blasts volumes without a spoken word.

25. "You matter to me"

Your small group is a segment of the whole ministry, but the students entrusted to you know they're genuinely loved, deeply cared for, and fully known from within. When they walk into a church service they may be one of many, but they know you know them. When they arrive at your group, they are greeted and loved by name—because they matter.

26. *"I'm proud of you"*

Some of the most empowering words you can say to a student are, "I'm proud of you." Someone other than their parent taking a genuine interest in their life can give them the confidence of an Olympic champion. You say, "I'm proud of you" through your actions every time you make a relational investment in their lives. (Although, don't let that take the place of an occasional verbal "way to go.")

140

Time spent building relationships will build trust and allow you to point them to Jesus.

"So now I am giving you a new commandment: Love each other. Just as I have loved you, you should love each other. Your love for one another will prove to the world that you are my disciples."

(John 13:34-35)

3 THOUGHTS ON CONNECTING WITH STUDENTS IN YOUR SMALL GROUPS

So you just signed up to be a small group leader. You got a little training, you're a tad nervous, and the first meeting of your small group is next week.

This might help get you thinking about the teenagers God has trusted to you during this next season of your youth ministry leadership. You can't do everything for every one, but you can do something.

27. Care for all (5)
If you were on my youth ministry team, you would be given somewhere between five and eight students to care for—and I'd ask you to care for all of them as well as you can. For the sake of illustration, lets assume you have five students. You care for them in simple ways; you know their names, are involved in their lives, and connect with them on a weekly basis. I want you to think

of yourself as the pastor of this little group of teenagers. The church may give someone else the official title of "youth pastor," but you have the unofficial title. You are the pastor to those kids.

28. **Pour into a few (3)**

Of the five students in your group, chances are good that you'll find three who will be regulars and really want what you have to relationally offer. Maybe it is a shared interest or a similar life story—either way, you just click with these three. So pour into them a little more than the others. When you're running an errand, ask one of them to join you so you can turn the mundane into ministry.

29. **Duplicate yourself in one (1)**

After about a month, ask God to show you the one student who you can really invest in. This may be the teenager you challenge to step up and lead the small group when you're gone. This is the person who you know you want to connect with outside of the group. Allow God to speak through you to shape this student into a great minister and future small group leader. Bottom line: this is the one kid within your group who gets the most of you.

Who will it be? You'll know!

Early in the small group year, try to figure out which of your group members you are going to really pour into... it can't be everyone.

If your gift is to encourage others, be encouraging. If it is giving, give generously. If God has given you leadership ability, take the responsibility seriously. And if you have a gift for showing kindness to others, do it gladly. Don't just pretend to love others. Really love them. Hate what is wrong. Hold tightly to what is good. Love each other with genuine affection, and take delight in honoring each other.

(Romans 12:8-10)

Welcome to the Club

The small group club consists of adults who love students for who they are and who they are becoming, not for the decisions they make. You probably didn't even know you joined a club, but you did.

Become a professional encourager. Every student (who am I kidding—every human) likes to be encouraged. If you don't learn anything else about being a small group leader, you need to learn how to encourage. Work hard to become a professional at affirmation. This will be difficult. Most students' decisions will make you want to kick a puppy rather than say something kind. Don't focus on the negative, instead be looking for something to celebrate in a teenager's life.

Fill your calendar with reminders. Show your interest by remembering the important things in a student's life. Birthdays are obvious, but what else is coming up that you can celebrate?

The school play, prom, or a driving test—these events are monumental in a teenager's life. Make an appearance when you can, but if you can't physically be there, be intentional about encouraging from a distance.

You can use your calendar as a prayer tool as well. Put a different student's name on each day of the week, or if a student asks for a specific prayer, add it to your calendar so you won't forget!

Be transparent. A student can tell when you are giving them the third degree on reading their Bible but you don't even know where yours is located. They may confuse Napoleon Dynamite with Napoleon Bonaparte, but they're not stupid and can figure out a fake adult real quick. Therefore, you gotta "practice what you preach."

Being a great small group leader is not about being a theologian, it is about doing life with students. The best way to teach a student how to have a relationship with Jesus is to have one and live it out.

I am not an expert, but I am in the trenches as a small group leader, and these are my three must-do tips. Make them your own, practice them, perfect them—and I promise next time I will teach you the club's secret handshake.

-Ryanne

Ryanne Witt is a very good small group leader, but she is incredible at finding and organizing small group leaders. I asked her to share a few things that make someone stand out as a great small group leader. Shoot for these, and you'll do just fine.

Since God chose you to be the holy people he loves, you must clothe yourselves with tenderhearted mercy, kindness, humility, gentleness, and patience. Make allowance for each other's faults, and forgive anyone who offends you. Remember, the Lord forgave you, so you must forgive others. Above all, clothe yourselves with love, which binds us all together in perfect harmony. And let the peace that comes from Christ rule in your hearts. For as members of one body you are called to live in peace. And always be thankful.

(Colossians 3:12-15)

Thoughts 30-68

THE BIG PICTURE

Small groups are best understood in the context of the whole youth ministry strategy. See how small groups are a key part of the discipleship process.

4 WAYS TO STAY IN TOUCH WITH STUDENT CULTURE

One of the biggest intimidations you may feel while serving students is the "age gap" between you and teenagers.

To be a great small group leader you don't have to be a youth culture expert. In fact, because youth culture is in constant evolution, keeping up with it is almost impossible, but understanding "enough" culture can be important and helpful. There are some ways you can stay in touch enough to know the issues without spending hours reading teen magazines, scouring Internet chat rooms, or breaking your neck trying a triple Ollie back flip at the skate park (not even sure that exists, but you get my point). Here are a few simple ways to stay in touch with teenage culture:

30. Browse youth culture websites
There are a few websites that will do the work of gathering up the highlights of student culture and present it to you in bite-sized portions.

Checkout sites like www.cpyu.org or www.understandingyouthculture.org to get up to speed on what is happening inside their world.

31. Tune in

What TV shows do your teenagers watch? If you don't know, ask them what they watch and then scan their shows. Don't tune out the commercials—pay attention to see what the world is trying to sell teenagers. This will help you understand their world, and it will give you illustration material to reinforce the points of your lessons using images, examples, and ideas already familiar to your students. (The Apostle Paul was the master of using the culture of his audience to teach them about God—see Acts 17:16-34.)

32. People watch

When you're at the mall or a local coffee shop, spend time watching, listening, and analyzing teenage behavior. Window shop at stores aimed at teenagers and grab a couple of teen magazines to further glimpse into their world.

33. Go social

Open an account on Facebook™ and add your students as friends. You can probably learn more about your students from Facebook™ in one week than you can from a semester of church attendance.

There are a couple of cautions here:

• You'll want to be extra careful that your Facebook™ posts exemplify the lifestyle and boundaries you want your students to keep. [See more on this topic on page 140.]

• You'll want to keep an arm's length distance from them (online). Don't comment on every status update they make (that's called a stalker) or use it as a tool to publicly call them out or hold them accountable (that's called a parent).

The bottom line: The more you understand the world that today's teenagers live in, the more effective your ministry will be to them. Technology, music, and clothes have changed, but the need for love, acceptance, and encouragement hasn't.

Popular music bands are here today, gone tomorrow. But love, care, and acceptance will always be in style.

Your eternal word, O Lord, stands firm in heaven. Your faithfulness extends to every generation, as enduring as the earth you created. Your regulations remain true to this day, for everything serves your plans.

(Psalm 119:89-91)

sMALL GRouP COVENANT

At the start of every small group year we ask students to sign a commitment form called the Small Group Covenant. The covenant provides students with an expectation of what small group is like, as well as our expectation of their behavior. Small groups will always have an element of fun, but they should also have some guidelines to ensure healthy community.

Here are the commitments:

CONSISTENT

I promise to regularly attend my small group. If I have to miss, I will take the responsibility to alert my small group leader.

COMPASSIONATE

I promise to be patient, loving, and forgiving toward my small group members because I understand that I am a part of a family of students who want to grow.

TEACHABLE

I joined this small group to grow spiritually, so I promise to do my part by listening attentively with an open heart and by bringing my Bible and notebook each week.

AUTHENTIC

I promise to be open and honest about my life with my small group at all times, allowing for accountability and encouragement between my small group and myself.

CONFIDENTIAL

I promise to honor my small group by not communicating what we discuss with anyone outside of our group.

Instead, we will speak the truth in love, growing in every way more and more like Christ, who is the head of his body, the church. He makes the whole body fit together perfectly. As each part does its own special work, it helps the other parts grow, so that the whole body is healthy and growing and full of love.

(Ephesians 4:15-16)

4 THINGS
YOU CAN EXPECT
FROM A SMALL GROUP

What can students expect from a small group? Try to focus on creating these four benefits when encouraging them to join a group:

34. Community
A small group of fellow Christians who encourage, challenge, and pray for one another.

35. Fellowship
It's easy for students to feel lost in the crowd. Small groups provide a more intimate environment for students, paving the way for deep friendships.

36. Bible study
At small groups, Bible studies can go more in-depth (because of discussion) than during other corporate teaching times.

37. A spiritual mentor

A loving adult leader from your ministry who, in addition to leading Bible study and discussion, will mentor students and promote spiritual growth.

140

Community, fellowship, Bible study, and mentoring: Work for these every week and your small group will be life-changing!

All the believers devoted themselves to the apostles' teaching, and to fellowship, and to sharing in meals (including the Lord's Supper), and to prayer. A deep sense of awe came over them all, and the apostles performed many miraculous signs and wonders. And all the believers met together in one place and shared everything they had. They sold their property and possessions and shared the money with those in need. They worshiped together at the Temple each day, met in homes for the Lord's Supper, and shared their meals with great joy and generosity—all the while praising God and enjoying the goodwill of all the people. And each day the Lord added to their fellowship those who were being saved.

(Acts 2:42-47)

4 THINGS TO KEEP IN MIND TO PICK THE PERFECT SMALL GROUP LOCATION

Where you meet as a small group is a big deal. Here are a few ideas to make sure you're picking a great location:

38. The perfect location has great meeting space to gather

Space is a critical concern of small groups—you want enough space to accomodate your style. For some, a table is the perfect place for a small group to meet. Others prefer the comfort of a living room. In some cases, which are less than ideal, you might choose a coffee shop or a restuarant, but those tend to be less comfortable and prone to more distractions. Whatever your environment, know that God will work in your group whether you're in a mansion or a shack, a coffee shop, or a family room. Just think it through and have a reason for why you chose it.

39. The perfect location is free of distractions

This is the most important aspect of a small group's meeting place. If you're meeting in a busy house with kids running around, phones ringing, dogs yelping, the game blaring on the TV, and Internet just a step away, your small group will lack focus. Distractions are community killers. When you're looking for the perfect small group location, make sure you have plenty of space and minimal distractions.

40. The perfect location isn't too far away from where students live

Proximity is a big deal. Putting groups together by schools and geography plays to their advantage. If you can cater to students' needs in this area, you'll make it easier for them to grow spiritually. Some groups will have a straggler who has to drive (that straggler might be the leader). Either way, choose the perfect location that is convenient for most and has an ideal environment.

41. The perfect location always has amazing snacks

You guessed it, the potential for good, teenage-friendly snacks should factor in which location you choose. Can Billy's mom cook? Do they have ample ice to keep the beverages cold? Will they cater Chick-fil-a® every week? Just kidding. Actually a great location is what matters most. You can always have small group members take turns bringing snacks, but if you can get a good location and good snacks, that's a win!

The right location is key, but don't hold up your small group ministry looking for perfection. If you don't get it right at launch, call it a "season," start a rotation, or keep looking.

9 WAYS TO CREATE A HEALTHY SMALL GROUP ATMOSPHERE

42. Get the location ground rules

Once you find your best-choice location, schedule a quick visit with the people who will be hosting the group. If you're meeting in a home, often they'll plan to be gone when you and your group are there, but it would be wise to find out their expectations firsthand. What parts of the house are off-limits? Which bathrooms should everyone use? Where can or can't students take food? Ask about parking to make sure students are parking in the right place. This meeting should happen several weeks in advance of your first meeting.

43. Be the first to arrive

Sometimes it can't be avoided, but arriving late can throw off the whole night. Being there before everyone else allows you to set the tone for the meeting and make sure everything is in place. If you are scrambling around and stressed out when the teenagers arrive, it can lead to a tough night.

44. Make sure your meeting area is set up

Look for distractions that need to be eliminated. Make sure the room is available and relatively clean and well lit. Turn off the TV/iPod/computer and think about placing a basket at the door for cell phones to minimize distractions. You can't go wrong with plenty of places to sit, too. Eliminate what you can—if the house has pets, make sure they're out of the area, unplug any house phones in the area, quarantine random siblings, and make sure any fancy "adult" art is off the walls (long story).

45. Sit at the same level as students

While as a leader you do control the night, keep the style of the night conversational by sitting with students and not above them. Make sure you keep the environment attentive, and don't allow students to lie down or all over each other.

46. Clearly communicate expectations to your students

Be sure to clearly communicate the house rules with students. The better you are at setting expectations and honoring the host home, the stronger your relationship with the host home will become.

It will also give you something to hold your students to when they cross the line.

47. Clean up messes

Have a great time at small group, but make sure you reset the room and clean up whatever mess has been created. If the host home family is gone, your goal should be for them to return home and wonder whether your group was even there. Make sure the students help out with all the tasks: reseting the room, cleaning up trash, throwing away leftovers, and putting furniture back (if it was moved). A nice touch is to take out their trash.

48. If anything goes wrong or gets broken, communicate with the lead youth worker

Your youth ministry is absolutely responsible for what happens in your host home environment during small group time. If you knock over a vase or students wrestle and shatter the lamp, don't let a frustrated parent surprise the church secretary the next day. Tell someone as soon as possible. You may even want to have the small group guys pay it back in some way, but whatever you do, keep the youth ministry in the loop... especially if a student carves their name in the furniture during prayer (yes, that's another long story).

49. Continue communicating with the host home

Give a copy of the small group calendar to the hosts so they know when they have a week off.

The more communication and fewer surprises between you and the hosts, the better.

50. Show appreciation with simple gifts

Encourage your students to thank the hosts after every meeting; maybe even consider leaving a little card for them on occasion. If possible, a small gift card can be super meaningful, or even a nice candle to help rid the family room of the "teenage boy" smell would be a great gesture.

Play nice with your host home—a great one is priceless. Love them and build a long-term partnership. Their ministry is hospitality.

51. Students may be intimidated

They may not know you. Many of them can think of 1,000 other things they would rather be doing. They may be as afraid as you are, but they'll do their best not to show it.

52. Students are hurting

Hiding is easier than exposing the truth. So right out of the gate, many students will test you to see if you will really love them. The tests can be painful or amusing, but failure to realize that they are simply tests of your love could result in deeper pain (for both of you).

53. Students need you to walk with them

No matter how intimidated they are or how hard they push away, know that each student was given to you by God for the next season of ministry. You might need to hold on to that truth in the weeks ahead.

You've been called to walk with a small group of students—they need you desperately. And someday, they might even acknowledge it, but don't hold your breath.

140

The first night of small groups can be one of the most difficult you'll face all year. Knowing this ahead of time is half the battle.

O Lord, you have examined my heart and know everything about me. You know when I sit down or stand up. You know my thoughts even when I'm far away. You see me when I travel and when I rest at home. You know everything I do. You know what I am going to say even before I say it, Lord. You go before me and follow me. You place your hand of blessing on my head. Such knowledge is too wonderful for me, too great for me to understand!

(Psalm 139:1-6)

Here are five parts of a typical small group. These don't happen each week and they don't always happen in order, but these are definitely elements that you'll want to regularly appear in your small groups.

54. Sharing life: Talk about life and hang out.

It feels most natural to start off a small group night with a relaxed atmosphere. Students usually show up over the span of the first 15 minutes of group, so some casual non-programmed time talking about a student's basketball game or a hilarious new YouTube™ video is usually time well spent. Plus, it'll give you an honest glimpse into what your students enjoy doing when they're not at group.

55. Accountability: Spend time sharing the good, bad, and ugly from your personal life.

Transition the time of hanging out into a time where you talk about the real-life stuff that's happening. If there's something you talked about the week before, that might make for a good transition; throw it out there. It doesn't have to be super serious—sometimes it will be and other times it will be random like a funny story everyone shares. Begin to focus the group and talk about personal discipleship decisions, Bible reading, girls/guys, purity, and relevant topics related to faith.

56. Teaching: Instruct and encourage students in their walk with God.

One of the purposes of a healthy small group is to learn biblical truths. Spend some time talking over a passage or biblical principle. The key to good teaching is helping teenagers think deeply and apply God's Word to their life.

57. Challenge: Ask them to take a step forward.

A good preparatory question to think about every week is, "How will I challenge them?" Maybe the challenge is a resource you want them to try. Maybe it is an article you read online and copied for them to read on their own.

Maybe it is a prayer you ask them to pray. Whatever it is, invite them to take a spiritual step every time you meet.

58. Prayer: Spend a few minutes in prayer for the members of your small group.

Cover the previous week's prayer requests quickly and then jump into what is currently on the hearts and minds of your group.

But don't just listen to God's word. You must do what it says. Otherwise, you are only fooling yourselves. For if you listen to the word and don't obey, it is like glancing at your face in a mirror. You see yourself, walk away, and forget what you look like. But if you look carefully into the perfect law that sets you free, and if you do what it says and don't forget what you heard, then God will bless you for doing it.

(James 1:22-25)

4 INSTANT
SMALL GROUP LESSONS TO PREP IN A PINCH

We've all done it—gone into small group unprepared or having prepped at the stoplight on the way to small group hoping God's Spirit shows up with an extra powerful dose. If you find yourself in a situation like this, here are four quick lessons you can probably share with little or no prep time:

59. Your life verse
Maybe there's a verse that your parents' dedicated you with as a child, or maybe there is a verse that you personally claimed during a particularly challenging season of your life. Either way, pull out that special verse and share the story about why it means so much and how you've experienced it in real life. Encourage others to share a key verse that has helped them in their walk with Jesus.

60. Your story
There is nothing more engaging than hearing someone's story of coming to Christ. It might be a good small group by just talking about when you

trusted Christ personally—your journey to faith. Others may also be willing to share, and you might be surprised at the discussion that follows about faith, unbelief, and even doubt. Just share your story and see what happens!

61. A life-changing moment

There's probably a spiritual moment in your life that has defined you. It could be a huge high or a dreadful low. Whether you share a joy or regret on this low-prep night, students will be riveted hearing how your life changed after that experience. Your failure stories (like wrecking your neighbor's Mercedes) will be particularly memorable, though an emotional experience (like holding your first child) can be just as meaningful.

62. Finding your spouse

Teenagers, especially girls, love to hear the stories of "how you met" your spouse. Share it and also include what you've learned of God's faithfulness. Even unmarried small group leaders have their own variation of this interesting story to share about their own relational journey.

Obviously, I hope you find time to prep your lesson each week, but when you're just having "one of those weeks" don't be afraid to try something different.

140 When you have your own personal quiet time, think about how you might need to share what you're currently learning.

JOSH'S LIFE VERSE: "But if you refuse to serve the Lord, then choose today whom you will serve. Would you prefer the gods your ancestors served beyond the Euphrates? Or will it be the gods of the Amorites in whose land you now live? But as for me and my family, we will serve the Lord."

(Joshua 24:15)

DOUG'S LIFE VERSE: The thief's purpose is to steal and kill and destroy. My purpose is to give them a rich and satisfying life.

(John 10:10)

6 TEACHING TIPS
TO HELP YOU HOLD THEIR ATTENTION

Healthy communication isn't guaranteed in your group time—you must actively pursue it. The following elements are not exclusive, but they weave together to help cast a compelling message. These are not about personal style, but rather tools in your arsenal to connect the audience to the message. Here are six ideas to get you going:

63. Humor

Laughter is one of the universal languages of humanity. Humor breaks down barriers and disarms people to accept truth. The highs of laughter make the serious points much more compelling. I love listening to people who can make me laugh yet cram truth down my throat at the same time. Try to use humor in some form every week—remember you don't have to be funny to use humor. You can start by not taking yourself so seriously and share some funny moments that you experienced throughout the week.

64. Authenticity

Find ways to inject yourself into the lesson to demonstrate the very real journey of following Christ. Unpack your life with your learnings, struggles, and flaws. Show that you are human and not always the hero at the end of every story.

65. Object lessons

Object lessons help connect students to a particular concept. Recently, we were talking about the debt we owe Christ and I dropped several nickels on the floor. These coins became a compelling image of forgiveness and debt. A few weeks before that, I used a little water-dropper to illustrate the world's love, and a large water pitcher to illustrate God's overflowing love for us. Object lessons don't need to be elaborate, just simple. Simple is both clear and memorable.

66. Using multiple senses

Don't allow students to just hear you teach. If you want half an hour of their attention, you must engage more than their ears. For example, if you're talking about Jesus turning water into wine, pour them a glass of Cabernet. Just kidding. But a lesson on the crucifixion could be accompanied by a large nail being passed around the group. Don't just use the ears, consider their sense of touch, smell, and sight, too.

67. Testimony
Students will typically pay better attention to story. When someone shares from their experience it's a great attention-getter. Invite a guest speaker to share a testimony that illustrates faith or the benefit received from choosing God's way.

68. Call to action
A great way to connect with your students is to call them to something much bigger than themselves. Show them what could be, and challenge them to take actions they didn't know they should take. Dare to challenge students to live a different life with practical actions connected to the teaching time.

More Than Just Bible Study

When my friend Mel and I chose to lead a small group, the first thing we decided was that we didn't want to lead a group entirely composed of "core" kids—those who had been raised in the church and knew the Bible better than we did. We wanted a mixture of core kids and "at-risk" kids who needed a little extra help. We also wanted to make it clear that when we gathered, it was to be more than just their Bible class; we wanted access to their lives. I've heard it said before, "People don't care how much you know, until they know how much you care," and that principle is the heartbeat of our small group.

Over a six-week time period the trust began to grow with our guys and slowly they began allowing us into their lives. We had also scheduled a "one-on-one" dinner with each of the guys to get to know them better.

In a calm setting without their peers around, we found they were more open about the real problems in their lives, what was working in their lives, and what areas they needed to change. We loved this opportunity to casually conduct a spiritual evaluation.

The first thing we noticed was that three out of four of our guys did not have a father or other positive male role model. We wanted that to change—at least the part we could change—the role model part. Because of this learning, we work on building up their self-esteem, we go to their swim meets and baseball games, we meet with them for lunch and text them during the week—all this to show them that we care about them and want to be there to support them.

We also partner with their parents to let them know we're also available for them if they need anything. We have had phone calls from parents who want us to talk to their kids about specific issues. We also have had phone calls from parents telling us how much they appreciate the positive change they see in their son. We always tell them it's not us; it is simply God choosing to work through us.

The most important action I've learned is to be open and ready to listen when God speaks to me and to allow God to use me. Some of the kids in our small group got there because I saw them at church and something urged me to go over and start a conversation. Within a short time I'd realize that God directed me to that particular teenager. When the kid opens up to me about what's wrong in his life and how he wants to change, I always follow up with, "You need to get connected to God and others who care for you—are you in a small group?"

As I'm writing this, one of our kids is giving his testimony this week. It's great to see him open his life and bare his emotional wounds for everyone to see so that he can help others with similar issues. It was also amazing that the rest of our small group decided that they were going to be there and support him so he was not on stage alone. God is truly working in these guys and I'm thankful every day that he allows me to be a part of the change in their lives!

-Matt

Matt Reynolds is a 50+ year old volunteer who has been a great small group leader. He works security in his day job and is drawn to kids on the edge. I asked him to share a little of his heart and vision for his small group guys, hoping that it would rub off on me—and maybe you, too.

But the Holy Spirit produces this kind of fruit in our lives: love, joy, peace, patience, kindness, goodness, faithfulness, gentleness, and self-control. There is no law against these things! Those who belong to Christ Jesus have nailed the passions and desires of their sinful nature to his cross and crucified them there. Since we are living by the Spirit, let us follow the Spirit's leading in every part of our lives. Let us not become conceited, or provoke one another, or be jealous of one another.

(Galatians 5:22-26)

GETTING INTO
STUDENTS' LIVES

Small groups are messy. Here are some ways to help get inside students' lives and what to do when you start dealing with tough stuff.

5 REMINDERS
WHEN COUNSELING STUDENTS

Relational ministry that's built on honesty and authenticity will lead to friendships that move deeper than the surface. Here are some reminders when you turn the corner and start to deal with some of the tougher stuff:

69. Be a focused listener

Making great eye contact and actively listening are an important first step in counseling a student. It reveals to the teenager that they are important to you. Do your best not to be surprised by what you hear, but make a genuine effort to care without judgment. It is a big deal that they're sharing with you! Be ready to listen and follow up with appropriate help. Caution: never promise that you won't share what's shared with you—it is a promise you can't keep when there are issues of harm, abuse, or addiction.

70. Don't quick-fix

Fight the urge to fix everything for them right away! Oftentimes, students know the right answer but need to talk it out to land on a solution. Once they do, give them some gentle nudging toward the correct choice, and encourage them to respond correctly to the situation.

71. Get them into the Bible

Point them to specific help in God's Word. Part of our job is to counsel and guide, but it is also to help students grow spiritually. It's OK if you're not a Bible expert; see if your church has a list of verses that you could study (on the subject you are counseling on), use Google to research the topic, or pull meaningful Scripture from your own study.

72. Share from your own experience

It often seems like God puts the right kids with the right leaders. As you're dealing with difficult issues, think about your own life and share from firsthand experience. Your authentic story will always be met with more receptivity.

73. Follow up as appropriate

If someone needs more help, schedule time to keep the conversation going. Don't be afraid to bring it up again, but be selective. No one responds well to nagging.

140

Most youth ministry counseling is "active listening"... when the issue is big, refer to a professional.

So let us stop going over the basic teachings about Christ again and again. Let us go on instead and become mature in our understanding. Surely we don't need to start again with the fundamental importance of repenting from evil deeds and placing our faith in God. You don't need further instruction about baptisms, the laying on of hands, the resurrection of the dead, and eternal judgment. And so, God willing, we will move forward to further understanding.

(Hebrews 6:1-3)

4 RESPONSES
WHEN A STUDENT SHARES
SOMETHING BIG

When a student in your small group opens up and shares a secret or a sin, many leaders have the instant tendency to panic or respond negatively. Here are four actions to take when you first hear the news:

74. Take a deep breath

Don't panic—set aside your own feelings of shock and try to make some clear-headed judgments. Stay calm; you can do this. In a weird way, this is what you were hoping would happen, that they would open-up their lives so your group could move below the surface.

75. Show up

Don't let a confession spook you away from helping students—unintentionally in busyness or intentionally because you're not sure how to handle it. Make sure you follow up with the student as soon as possible. Leaving them hanging may trigger regret and fear. They may regret sharing the secret with you and second-guess any further transparency. Your feedback is essential to their healing process. It also helps them realize they are loved and accepted despite their sin. They don't need you to absorb their problem as your own; they just want you to help direct them to a path of peace.

76. Go to God

Pray, pray, pray. Never underestimate the power of God to work in this situation. Beg for his wisdom. When my pastor talks about prayer, he says, "Prayer can do what God can do." Commit to seeking his power and presence in your life and in the life of the teenager.

77. Team up

You are not alone in this! Talk with your youth leader or a veteran small group leader to help guide you through this situation.

140 A confession is a gift of trust from one of your small group members. Handle it with care—God is going to use you!

Confess your sins to each other and pray for each other so that you may be healed. The earnest prayer of a righteous person has great power and produces wonderful results.
(James 5:16)

THE 4 STEPS FOR DEALING WITH A STUDENT'S ABUSE OR NEGLECT

Most small group leaders won't feel equipped to deal effectively with a student in imminent danger of abuse or neglect. It's a scary scenario to address. However, hoping to avoid your initial discomfort by avoiding the issue can cause tragic life-long pain in a student's life. The great news is that these events are rare and after you deal with one, you will feel prepared for others in the future.

While you are trusted to handle most of the typical situations with discernment, there is the chance a student will reveal something beyond your ability. In extremely serious situations use these four steps to respond to a major crisis:

78. STEP 1: Alert the student
After counseling and consoling the student, let him know you have the responsibility to get help for the situation; part of that help will require

privately making a couple of people aware of what happened. While we still very much agree to the covenant that includes confidentiality, a small group leader should not promise to "never tell anyone" about certain things a student may share. In some cases, you simply must break confidence to best help the teenager. Let him know that you will walk with him through every step of getting him the help he needs. Be sure to communicate your care for him and a strong desire to make sure he is safe.

Be prepared for the student to sternly object to getting help; do your best to ease his fear. Do not let the student talk you out of taking the next step. Just encourage him, and let him know he will not go through this alone. If he refuses to start the process, let him know you will begin the process of getting help without him.

79. STEP 2: Partner with the student and family

Get in contact with your lead youth worker immediately—these situations are never easy to handle, and the lead youth worker will be there to help you through it. Someone "above your pay grade" can help you decide if this situation requires filing a report with authorities. They will also discuss further action with you. Even if you aren't sure this is "big enough" to warrant reporting to authorities, partner with the church so they can pray for you and help you better care for the teenager.

80. STEP 3: Report to the authorities

After partnering with your lead youth worker, fill out the necessary reports together to begin the process. You're not expected to be a professional in handling this; don't worry if there are questions you cannot answer.

81. STEP 4: Follow further instructions

The church should be able to instruct you on what steps, if any, need to be taken from here. Most likely, your role in the reporting of the situation will be complete at this

What if it turns out the student told you false information?

You can only act on information they give to you. Students may make false accusations to retaliate against parents or authority figures. The consequences will be up to the student to bear. You must move forward as if they are being truthful until you know for certain they aren't.

point; it would be rare for your involvement to be required beyond the initial report. Continue to pray for people involved in the situation and pray that it will be resolved quickly. You will, however, want to follow up with the student as he or she travels the scary path of getting help.

Again, these steps should only be followed in the cases of abuse or serious neglect.

"Give justice to the poor and the orphan; uphold the rights of the oppressed and the destitute. Rescue the poor and helpless; deliver them from the grasp of evil people."
(Psalm 82:3-4)

Handling discipline is never easy. First, determine who really needs to be corrected. If it's a group problem, address it as a group. If it's a couple of people, pull them aside together. If it's an individual issue, address the individual. Here are a few ways to handle discipline issues:

82. Pull them aside

Don't pull off a major correction in front of the entire small group; make sure you pull people aside after group time and begin a conversation. If you are fortunate enough to have a co-leader and the situation is distractive enough, the co-leader could remove the student and have a corrective conversation.

83. Be clear on what they're doing wrong

Address the problem directly. If it is causing a problem with the whole group, help the student to see how his or her actions are distracting everyone.

Usually a student will know, but some are so self-absorbed, they don't realize how they are affecting those around them.

84. Show grace
Be quick to model grace. Be strong and firm, but follow quickly with extra love and grace. The more seasoned the youth worker, the easier it is to show grace. If you are new to youth ministry, carefully temper your response. I will usually say something like, "You can never do that again in our small group. I love you, but that was inappropriate and unacceptable. Cool? You know I love you, right?" Sometimes solving a behavioral issue will be that simple.

85. Look for and encourage correct behavior
When you see appropriate behavior, make sure you comment on it and encourage the student when he or she has a good night. Your affirmation will be meaningful and restorative. Chances are high that what is encouraged will be repeated.

86. Follow up later after a set amount of time
If appropriate, set a follow-up date to make sure that the student has made the appropriate changes. Use this time to build a stronger

relational connection; this bond may prevent it from happening again—or if it does happen again, you'll have an open, relational door to help correct the behavior.

If you listen to constructive criticism, you will be at home among the wise. If you reject discipline, you only harm yourself; but if you listen to correction, you grow in understanding. Fear of the Lord teaches wisdom; humility precedes honor.

(Proverbs 15:31-33)

2 REASONS NOT TO REMOVE A STUDENT FROM SMALL GROUP

There are legitimate reasons for removing a student from your small group—and there are some other reasons that may feel right but may be more harmful than helpful. Here are a couple I've seen in the past few years in our ministry:

87. The student isn't showing up

Just because a student isn't showing up doesn't mean you should let them go—it actually means you might have an opportunity to go the extra mile to care for them. Be faithful to call and check up, even if it feels futile. A student's absence can become a pastoral opportunity. We divide our youth group into smaller groups for this very reason: so everyone will be cared for and missed when they don't attend. Don't give up on them yet! Your next call or text could be more meaningful than you will ever know. For example, after months of following up with one "always gone" student, he finally began attending my small group. He said it was the occasional effort on my part that finally made him come back.

88. The student doesn't seem to care about the group

If we removed students every time they were dejected or apathetic, we wouldn't have very many teenagers left in small groups. Consider apathy a sign of an unmet need and consider yourself the "pastoral detective" to figure out what it is. Finding that need and trying to meet it is one of the marks of a good youth worker.

140

Don't be too quick to remove a student from your group. Be longsuffering and care for them before jumping the gun.

So then, since we have a great High Priest who has entered heaven, Jesus the Son of God, let us hold firmly to what we believe. This High Priest of ours understands our weaknesses, for he faced all of the same testings we do, yet he did not sin. So let us come boldly to the throne of our gracious God. There we will receive his mercy, and we will find grace to help us when we need it most.

(Hebrews 4:14-16)

∃ REASONS

TO REMOVE A STUDENT FROM YOUR SMALL GROUP

We wish it didn't have to happen, but from time to time it simply has to—you've got to remove a disruptive member from your small group. You just read some reasons NOT to remove a student from your small group, but here are a few reasons it might be time.

89. Major disruption

Sometimes the entire group suffers because of the misbehavior of one, and that simply can't continue for a small group to succeed. Some disruption is normal; don't penalize a teenager for not having all the needed social skills, instead coach them on how to be an effective participant in a group environment. But, if that doesn't work and a student is still a consistent source of distraction (and you've made enough attempts to make it better), it might be time for more severe measures. Part of the removal process should be rerouting the student to another small group. Remember, this teenager is redeemable; he just needs another opportunity to succeed in a different environment. Another leader may be able to help where you have been unable.

This is the nature of ministry and the value of having a diverse team of adults who are leading small groups.

90. Conflict

Conflict can be healthy, but at some point it can destroy the group. If you're having continued and draining conflict with the parents and their expectations of the small group (or because of a student's expectations of the group), help the teenager relocate to another group. Like with disruption, some conflict is normal, but too much can hurt everyone.

91. "Fit"

This is one of those rare, "only-break-in-case-of-emergency" options. This one is ambiguous, and if you're not very careful, it can become the "catchall" to remove a student for personal or political reasons. Usually, you'll know after a few meetings whether they fit or not. Have a conversation and give the student permission to seek out a new group where he or she may fit better. But please, be careful with this one because it's easy for it to backfire and explode on you.

While I would rather help the student adjust and learn to interact better, I'd rather move her to a new group if the efforts aren't working for her and are hindering the group from growing together. I would not, however, remove her from the group unless there is a specific place for her to go that will be more of a "win."

Every small group will usually have at least one "extra-grace-required" kid in their small group. Be patient and long-suffering and ask God to make it clear if a student genuinely needs to be removed from your group. The goal should be to

When transplanting a student to a group that's a better fit, you'll do well to discuss it with other small group leaders first. Consider finding a leader whose group is a better match. Once the leader shows an interest in that student, arrange some opportunities for them to connect. After the student is comfortable with the potential new leader, bring up the idea of making the switch. By doing this, you turn a potentially painful and rejection-laden transition into a positive scenario. Everybody wants to be wanted. Set the teenager up for a great transition by orchestrating a clean handoff.

always "repot" a student where they can connect and grow.

If one student is ruining small group for everyone, remove him or her. Discipline is an essential part of discipleship.

But you, O Lord, are a God of compassion and mercy, slow to get angry and filled with unfailing love and faithfulness.

(Psalm 86:15)

HOW TO REMOVE A STUDENT FROM YOUR SMALL GROUP

You hate to have to do it—but sometimes you have to remove a student from your small group. Here are some ideas (that aren't simple) to help you in the process from start to finish:

92. Share expectations and give boundaries right from the beginning

It's not good to allow one student to ruin something for the whole group. I like the "3 Strikes Rule" myself—it gives you a chance for some warnings before drastic measures have to be taken. Put the power to win or lose in the students' actions. If they want to be in the group, they'll act like it. At the end of group time, if someone has really blown it, let him or her know they've got a strike against them and they need to adjust their behavior before they return. Go public with your plan, and consider giving everyone back a "strike" at the halfway point of the small group year. Bottom line: Be grace-filled but firm and consistent with your boundaries. You are the shepherd and you want to keep the sheep from hurting one another.

93. Talk to the student directly when there's a problem

Removing a student from a small group should never surprise a teenager. Talk to the problem student when you first see a warning sign, and coach him or her to the correct behavior. Keep in constant communication with the student so they know they are failing to meet your expectations and where they stand. Don't bring the other members of your small group into the correction, with the exception of perhaps an acknowledgment that you are working toward a resolution.

94. Ask them to take a couple weeks off

Before you remove them completely, consider giving them a few weeks off to recalibrate their thoughts and behavior. You'd be amazed at how powerful a "time-out" can be for them (as well as how your group will respond when they hear what went down).

95. Keep in communication with the leadership

Inform the lead youth worker of the history of your small group and what you've done to help resolve the situation. Ask for insight, prayer, and follow your leader's advice. Your leader may try to move the kid to a different group to see if a "change in scenery" brings a change of heart.

96. **Engage the parents**

Don't let a decision so important (and potentially volatile) be done in isolation. Talk to mom and dad through the process and partner with them in helping the student's behavior change for the better. If you can engage them during the time-out stage, it'll really help if/when you have to remove the student altogether. (Obviously, this assumes the parent(s) cares... which isn't always the case).

97. **If all else fails, remove the student and ask them to consider small groups next year**

If all else has failed and a student needs to be permanently removed, please leave the door open for next year. A lot can change in a year, and you can pray they'll take it more serious next time.

We hate it, but sometimes you just have to ask them to leave.

The Heart of Small Group

The heart of small groups is relationships—the conduit of everything that happens in small groups. The condition of the group (healthy, dysfunctional, spiritually growing, stuck-in-fun mode) is an indication of the relationships within the group. The quality of relationships can inhibit or promote the group's effectiveness, quality, and level of joy.

Healthy groups can get a bad rap for being cliques when their thriving relationships extend beyond the weekly meeting. Their camaraderie is so rich that they not only study the Bible together, they genuinely enjoy doing life together. Unfortunately, the opposite is also true of groups with poor relationships. They are like a train wreck—a smoldering heap of unhappiness, bent out of shape, and not a place anybody wants to be.

Because relationships can bring joy, apathy, or anguish to small groups, **leaders must be strategic about building relational ties within the group.** If we allow the relationships to take their natural course, the tendency will be for the group to sour. Creating memorable and meaningful moments for your small group can open the door to sharing on a deep level, personal healing, lasting connections, and spiritual growth.

Unfortunately, despite your best efforts, conflict can make its way into any small group. Depending on how the leader deals with the relational strife, it can actually be an opportunity for growth. **A mark of good leadership is turning relational conflict into a teachable moment.** A group that is willing to admit, discuss, and resolve animosity is on fertile ground for spiritual growth.

I learned this lesson when Carl punched Jesse (two guys in my small group) in the face one day at school. My immediate thought was, "teachable moment." Although, if I had been there when it happened, my first thought might have been "duck," then "teachable moment." Rather than allowing this to become a relationship-killer, I jumped at the chance to teach relational conflict-resolution skills and bring restoration to the group.

After talking to each of the boys separately, I had them meet me for dinner. There was an awkward feeling as they sat together on the opposite side of the table from me (with all the tension in the air, the word "duck" came back to mind). I imagined the meal ending with napkin holders and plates of pasta shooting through the air as the boys rumbled through this Italian restaurant, ending with a high repair bill and more tension. However, we had an amazing discussion about the conflict, relationships, and healthy resolution.

At one point, I had to step outside to take an important phone call. Fearful of returning to a restaurant engulfed in flames, I was surprised to find the boys laughing about what happened.

My learning through this episode? I need to take the relationship development of my small group serious. You do, too. Don't let nature take its course with such a foundational aspect of your group. If you do, some will be left out, others will tear members down, somebody's going to get de-friended on Facebook™, and it's going to be ugly. Diligently incorporate healthy relational elements into your group. Being proactive about building relationships within your group **will create fertile ground for God's work to flourish.**

-Dennis

Dennis Beckner has been a small group leader on our team for many years. He's a good friend and loves volunteer youth ministry so much that he blogs at www.VolunteerYouthMinistry.com.

PRACTICAL TIPS FOR A SUCCESSFUL SMALL GROUP

This section takes on common questions and offers practical advice to help your small group thrive.

5 WAYS TO ENCOURAGE SMALL GROUP STUDENTS TO TAKE A NEXT STEP

Here are five ways small group leaders can help teenagers grow spiritually on their own:

98. Think about the individual

A large group setting usually has a more objective, big-picture look at Scripture that creates opportunities to challenge students in the crowd. The small group setting is usually more subjective, allowing students to be challenged individually in a setting where they are personally known and can be passionately cared for. Small group leaders can hone in on the individual and have a good feel for each student's spiritual temperature. Because of that, they are qualified to prescribe spiritual resources that will challenge and help students develop specific spiritual disciplines.

A helpful exercise for small group leaders is to mentally replay discussions that have happened with students in your small group over the past month. Those discussions should reveal some areas of spiritual strength and struggle. If your conversations haven't given you more insight to a teenager's spiritual condition, it might be wise to reconsider the types of questions you are asking. How is a teenager better because of your conversations or how are you better equipped as a leader to help them grow spiritually?

99. Personalize a resource

When you find the right resource that will help them grow on their own, take time to personalize it with an encouraging note. Make it personal and specific. Share you heart and explain why you want him to use the resource and what benefit you hope he gains. When you hand a resource to someone, it communicates you care about him personally and that you are actively working to help him grow spiritually. It doesn't have to be a fancy or expensive resource to be a helpful one.

100. Encourage big and little steps

In our ministry, we try to celebrate any step forward in one's spiritual journey. A baby-step is still a step forward. Sometimes we have to remember that each student experiences spiritual growth at his or her own pace. For some students small steps are huge milestones. For other students, they require a bigger challenge that will stretch them beyond baby-steps. At first, they might not believe it's possible, but if they feel like you believe in them they'll be more likely to accept the challenge. Think of teenagers in terms of their spiritual potential rather than their current destination. Just remember to encourage any step, no matter the size.

101. Offer to go through the study/book/ resource with them

What if you worked through a resource alongside your students? Help them know you are serious about their spiritual growth and you will walk down the path with them. Here are a few ways you might do that:

- Read a few chapters with them.

- Serve with them in ministry for a few weeks while they test-drive different opportunities.

- Text them with questions and thoughts about what they are reading.

The concept of "growing on your own" doesn't release us from helping students grow spiritually. We set them up for success when we help them get started. Like training wheels on a bike, you back off once they're confident and able to continue without your constant support and supervision.

102. Follow up in a few weeks to encourage them

Building teenagers up and releasing them to grow is good leadership. Giving resources away to help them grow on their own is a great way to get them moving in the right direction. But better leadership appears when you offer some accountability by checking up on their progress. Accountability encourages an expectation and expresses that you are partnering with them in their spiritual journey. This is more about celebrating the win than highlighting the weakness. I find that when I focus on the good, students become empowered to pick up the slack where they're lacking.

Next steps in spiritual growth aren't easy, but they can be life-transforming opportunities and small group leaders can be the architect to change.

140 There is a direct link between small groups and discipleship. Challenge your students to take spiritual steps throughout the year!

So I say, let the Holy Spirit guide your lives. Then you won't be doing what your sinful nature craves. The sinful nature wants to do evil, which is just the opposite of what the Spirit wants. And the Spirit gives us desires that are the opposite of what the sinful nature desires. These two forces are constantly fighting each other, so you are not free to carry out your good intentions.

(Galatians 5:16-17)

From Pimples to Prom

What do you do with a bunch of seventh-grade boys who you have never met before? This is what I encountered six years ago as a started my journey in youth ministry. What would I say? Would they like me? Would I do a good job? All of these ideas ran through my mind. Well, I survived that first meeting and now the hundreds that followed. Being transparent, real, and available has truly helped the guys grow closer to Christ and to each other.

At first I thought that I should be just a teacher, giving these students the greatest sermons they have ever heard. Quickly I found that my group didn't want a teacher—they wanted an older brother. Because they didn't know me, I had to tell them about myself. I let them know I was human, that I had messed up (big time), and that I was still a work in progress. This led the way for real sharing and growth.

By sharing with them my own struggles and failures, it allowed them to open up to the group and reveal theirs. By no means was this an overnight sensation. This process took about two years. During their freshman year of high school, our discussions went to a deeper level. We shared real struggles. We transitioned from a "Sunday school class" to an open group discussing real-life struggles, not just giving "Bible answers" to "Bible stories." Text messages of support and prayer requests were flying back and forth and it was both powerful and rewarding.

I have some of the greatest conversations with the guys in my group outside of our programmed time, whether we are shooting hoops or sharing frozen yogurt. Not racing home to watch the news or check my e-mail has proven to be of great help as I'm now more present. Being available in their environment has built the bonds that I know will last a lifetime.

These boys, now turning into men, have become part of my family. We aren't just a Bible study/small group that meets on Wednesday nights from 7 to 9 p.m.—we are family. They call my wife "mom," they come over for breakfast, we surf together, we talk on the phone, and they attend my children's sporting events. As "family," we are all growing closer to Christ together.

-Paul

Paul Coppes has volunteered "for the cycle" in our ministry. That means he came into youth ministry as a small group leader to seventh-grade boys and finished with them as seniors. It is a huge accomplishment!

103. Pray for your small group members

Pray for your students every week! You do the possible and ask God to do the impossible in their lives. Creating a list of their prayer requests during small group will help you remember to follow up on how God is answering prayers and give you something to talk about every week.

104. Prepare to teach your small group lesson

A good small group leader doesn't arrive to small group unprepared to teach (or facilitate the discussion). Be sure to carve out some time to prepare. The earlier in the week you prepare, the fewer times you'll be caught off guard by a difficult-to-grasp Scripture, issue, or oddly written curriculum. You'll also avoid the last-minute scramble for illustrations and application. Good preparation will always lead to better discussion.

105. Let God's Spirit lead you during your small group time

Be prepared to teach the lesson, but if you sense God doing something, move with it. Don't hide behind the Spirit and be unprepared, but don't fight the Holy Spirit stirring either. Other legitimate factors that may justify ditching your lesson may include:

For the extremely rare occasion you show up to small group unprepared because life got a little too hectic, keep a copy of page 59 in your small group binder for last-minute, in-a-pinch lessons you can do on the fly.

- **Crisis in a student's life**—allow the group to minister to each other.

- **Questions about Christian living**—anytime students are asking questions about spiritual issues, a leader should weigh out the competing values: Do you finish the curriculum? Do you pause and address the students' questions? Can you do both? Only you can adequately answer that question.

106. Seek out the one

Be on the lookout for students who may need special attention. The signs can be subtle; they are more quiet than usual, more high-strung, or they use a word that hints at a repressed feeling or secret. Chances are good that someone will be a little needier each week.

When you get a feeling a student needs some special attention, you're probably on to something. Seek out that student for a follow-up one-on-one conversation during the week.

107. Direct students toward next steps
Remember, the small group is an open door to discipleship. Challenge your students to take a next step by growing on their own and serving in a ministry. Don't forget to praise them as they follow through.

108. Follow up with students who missed small group
A short text or call goes a long way. Make quick contact with the students who missed. Maybe the door will open to a significant conversation, and at the very least they'll feel cared for. When you call, use their home phone number so one of the parents might answer. This parental opportunity can create a great chance to brag on their kid while you have their attention—that's great youth ministry.

140 There's a lot to juggle as a small group leader. You can't go wrong if you focus on prayer and care.

The Lord is righteous in everything he does; he is filled with kindness. The Lord is close to all who call on him, yes, to all who call on him in truth.

(Psalm 145:17-18)

109. Grab a soda or coffee with a student
Make it a goal to visit with one student outside of your small group one time a month. The extra care and attention is vital to the depth of your relationships—conversation outside of group is a big deal, make the most of it!

110. Connect with the youth ministry leader
Spending a few minutes connecting with the youth ministry leader is important so everyone is aware of needs, expectations, and changes. Even a simple e-mail to keep him or her in the loop on the good, bad, and ugly of your small group is critically important. Be sure to also pass along a great ministry moment you had with a student or witnessed within the ministry. That, and a word of appreciation toward the leader, should be part of every conversation (the lead youth worker needs a little encouragement, too).

111. **Write notes**

Mail that arrives in an envelope is so rare these days that it's very meaningful. There's so much power in the written word. Teenagers may be so surprised that they will keep the letter as a prized possession. Not only that, parents will probably see the card/postcard when it arrives in the mail and will be encouraged, too. Their hearts will be warmed to know their child is being loved, cared for, and challenged spiritually. Beyond that, parents will be relieved to know they have you on their team diligently working to mold their sons and daughters into Christ-followers.

112. **Plan a fun night out**

Do some sort of fun group activity outside of your normal small group time. It doesn't have to be fancy, simple works: go miniature golfing, play video games, toilet paper the pastor's house—do something fun that will create a lasting memory.

The group that plays together stays together! Remember, the more quality time you spend with students, the more they will feel a part of the group and the more you'll have access to their lives.

113. Serve together

Consider participating in a service project as a small group. Find a needy family in the church, work with a local food bank, or make plans to serve in a church-wide event. Bonding happens when you serve together.

> The strategy here is to build stronger relationships and create a reference point for students to look back on when life gets difficult. Those they've bonded with will be the ones they go to for help.

We know what real love is because Jesus gave up his life for us. So we also ought to give up our lives for our brothers and sisters. If someone has enough money to live well and sees a brother or sister in need but shows no compassion—how can God's love be in that person? Dear children, let's not merely say that we love each other; let us show the truth by our actions. Our actions will show that we belong to the truth, so we will be confident when we stand before God.

(1 John 3:16-19)

HOW TO PRAY FOR YOUR SMALL GROUP

Pray for your students to feel God's love and acceptance. The teenage years aren't typically kind to self-esteem. Pray that your students discover their identity in Christ, and in him alone.

114. Pray for wisdom in how to demonstrate and model love to each student in your group. Every teenager is unique and needs you to speak their unique love-language. Pray that God will make your love for them evident.

115. Pray for your students to make Christ-like choices and for purity to characterize them. Of all the challenges for teenagers, peer pressure is still very strong. Pray that God will be number one in their life.

116. **Pray for their issues;** family struggles, personal decisions, pressures, addictions, friendship conflicts, and so on. And pray that in all these issues they will open their life to God's Word.

Praying for your students will help your own heart be spiritually sensitive to their needs. Prayer is time well spent.

Then Jesus said to the disciples, "Have faith in God. I tell you the truth, you can say to this mountain, 'May you be lifted up and thrown into the sea,' and it will happen. But you must really believe it will happen and have no doubt in your heart. I tell you, you can pray for anything, and if you believe that you've received it, it will be yours. But when you are praying, first forgive anyone you are holding a grudge against, so that your Father in heaven will forgive your sins, too."

(Mark 11:22-25)

RANDOM
REMINDERS

This is the equivalent of a miscellaneous section. Stuff we wanted to share, but didn't know where else to put it. Some of our favorite material is in this section.

Healthy youth ministries have healthy teams. Here are some thoughts about the importance of unity within your team:

117. A unified vision makes for an impactful ministry

A great small group leader is unified with the vision of the youth ministry and aligned with the purposes and goals of the church. If you're not on board with the vision, please help the health of your church and either get on board, or get off the bus. Personal agendas birth divisiveness and impede a ministry's movement toward health.

Even good agendas can conflict with the vision and be divisive. You can make suggestions about the direction of the ministry, but your job is to lead within the role and boundaries ultimately decided by the lead youth worker.

If you can't follow the agenda now, remove yourself and return at a time when the ministry is heading in a direction you can support.

118. A unified team focuses on changed people rather than church politics

Interpersonal issues, personality conflicts, and church drama distract us from our all-important mission to walk with students. We are called to be relational and a spiritual influence to teenagers. Allowing your focus to be diverted by distractions robs your students of a focused leader. Rise above the noise and simply serve the teenagers within your small group.

119. A unified heart is led by God's Spirit

A heart that is united with the church and student ministry isn't distracted by problems. There will always be problems.

When a ministry is ensnarled in strife, selfishness is present somewhere as it's the root of most problems. When we don't get what we think is right or best, the sulking, outbursts, resignations, and visits to complain to the senior pastor begin. Remember that the youth leader is put in place to provide vision and strategy. As difficult as it may be at times, align yourself under that vision for the greater good of the ministry. You may discover that your way, though good, was not the best path for reaching the end goal.

I appeal to you, dear brothers and sisters, by the authority of our Lord Jesus Christ, to live in harmony with each other. Let there be no divisions in the church. Rather, be of one mind, united in thought and purpose.

(1 Corinthians 1:10)

WHAT TO DO IF THE LINE BETWEEN **LEADER** AND **FRIEND** IS BLURRED

Imagine: the line between small group leader and friend has blurred. Instead of being a responsible leader, you're now just "one of the guys." When this happens, respect drops. Your role as adult leader is compromised. Now what?

Well, it happens—please realize you're not the first person to fall prey to this trap. Here's a few items to restoring your rightful place as a loving adult leader:

120. Analyze the situation
How did this "blurring" happen? What's your role here? Have you done something that triggered this change? Were you lax in discipline or overly interested in being accepted? Were you focused too much on humor and hanging-out rather than leading them into deep discussion and spiritual depth? What happened to the respect level after that situation? Do you need to ask for forgiveness?

Are you just being run over? Figure out how you got there so you can get out of it and avoid getting stuck there again.

121. Talk to a trusted few

It's wise to talk to a few of the students in your group and cast a vision of how you want to change and why you need their help and support. Explain that you want to have fun and be friendly, but you also want to be able to turn the corner into deeper conversations.

- **Have "the talk" with your entire small group** and make sure the ones who you talked to first are modeling agreement to the others in the group.

- **Apologize if necessary.** Humility and authenticity always win.

- **Share your vision and heart for them** and how a healthy relationship with them is critical for everyone to keep growing.

- **Set boundaries** you and your students will follow to maintain each of your roles.

- **Show them the path** toward getting back to a healthy place: "I think it's time for us to move to a deeper place..." or "this group is more than hanging-out and having a good time..." or "it's probably my fault for not pushing us enough and playing too much..."

122. Be the leader

This is the time when you will have to lean a little on the leader side of the continuum and less on the friend side. After a course correction, be strong and faithful and lead your group. Have fun, but keep a watchful balance to make sure the lines are clear. Guard your decisions so that "a leadership blur" doesn't happen again. Leading isn't easy, but you'll figure it out!

God has given each of you a gift from his great variety of spiritual gifts. Use them well to serve one another. Do you have the gift of speaking? Then speak as though God himself were speaking through you. Do you have the gift of helping others? Do it with all the strength and energy that God supplies. Then everything you do will bring glory to God through Jesus Christ. All glory and power to him forever and ever! Amen.

(1 Peter 4:10-11)

WHAT TO DO WHEN YOU MESS UP

It wasn't that long ago a small group leader in our ministry called to talk about a big mistake he had made. It involved a group of guys, Buffalo wings, and a little restaurant called... Hooters. The next few hours after that phone call were critical—we were fortunate that it was an experienced volunteer who followed these steps to re-establish trust with the parents of his small group. (By the way, most parents don't view Hooters as a "family restaurant.") Here's what we did:

123. Own it without excuses

When you make a mistake, own it! Honesty and openness are essential for rebuilding trust with the offended party. The last thing you want to do is to minimize what happened and pretend it isn't a big deal. It is a big deal, and it needs an owner. You committed the foul, so take your lumps.

124. Apologize for what you've done and start over

So you've been honest about what happened; now it is time to apologize for it and admit you were wrong. This isn't going to be easy, but it is a sign of humility, repentance, and your humanity. Don't try to appear perfect... it doesn't set a realistic example for your students to follow.

125. Earn trust back one good decision at a time

It might take some time, but try not to repeat the same bad decision and continue to make good decisions. You are a leader and it is time to get back to leading again. One good decision is to give detailed plans of your intentions with teenagers at least a week in advance. This will give parents an opportunity to address concerns and gain peace of mind that your plans are sound.

126. Keep in mind: The longer you've served and the more relational deposits you've made into the "longevity bank," the more you will be trusted despite an occasional mess up. Also, keep in mind, messing up does happen—you won't be the first.

WHAT TO DO WHEN ONLY A COUPLE STUDENTS SHOW UP

You're thinking about canceling group tonight because it looks like only one student is going to show up. Don't be so quick to gong the night—it could become a great opportunity for real good ministry.

127. Be thankful

Don't be discouraged, this is a blessing in disguise! It's a great opportunity to pour into one student. Don't think of it as a miss, instead think about it as if God gave you this divine appointment. Great memories, relational depth, and transformational trust can come out of "almost cancelled" small group sessions.

When you cancel on the one student who was planning to attend, it can send a negative message about his or her worth. So, instead send just the opposite message by getting together and doing something memorable.

THEN

128. Drop the lesson and go 1-on-1

This is not the time to cram the lesson down the throat of the one student brave enough to actually show up. Have a significant conversation and see what God is doing in his or her life. Look for opportunities to challenge this student in a specific area of weakness or opportunity.

OR

129. Ditch the meeting and go out for a treat

Call the home you're meeting at and tell them that group is off for the night—you're taking it to the coffee shop, batting cages, or Yarn Barn instead. Give everyone a night off and have some fun.

One-on-one time should be one of your goals as a small group leader. Don't cancel group if there's just one—take advantage of it!

Be You—Let Them Be Themselves

Be yourself, celebrate your uniqueness. It takes courage to be who God created you to be, flaws and all. My guys know that I am not perfect. I work on being authentic every time we meet. I want them to see the real me and be inspired to be themselves as well. Kids have a lot of pressure to conform in school. It is refreshing to see someone who doesn't go along with the crowd and has the courage to live for Christ no matter what the crowd is doing. Also, small group should be a place where your kids don't have to be ON. It's hard for them to do that if YOU are always ON. I allow them to see my ups and downs and see how Christ works in both circumstances.

Make sure that you are growing in your walk with God. I can't expect my small group guys to grow if I'm not growing myself. One morning during my quiet time I was praying that my guys would grow to know and trust God in a deep, powerful way. I felt God telling me that if I would just focus on putting him first and growing in my relationship with him that he would take care of my guys. Being a small group LEADER requires leading the guys in their walk with God. In order to do that, you also have to be stepping out and pushing forward in your relationship with God. They can't follow you if you ain't goin' anywhere.

Remember that you are investing in eternity when you are investing in the lives of your teenagers. If they can develop a solid relationship with God while they are young, they will make the right choices as they go throughout their lives. Some of the best ministry time is when you are just hanging out. I like to go watch their football games or take them with me when I run errands. If you let them into your life, they are more likely to let you into theirs. They have met my family and friends. I don't want to compartmentalize them into 90 minutes every Tuesday night. They call, we text, we grab a bite when we can. These relationships, I hope, will last for a lifetime and on into eternity.

-Chip

I've literally been to Africa and back with Chip Bragg. I asked this key volunteer to write down some essentials for a healthy small group leader. I loved what he shared and hope it inspires you, too!

6 DO'S AND DON'TS OF SMALL GROUP MINISTRY

130. DO your best to remember names

What, you're not good at remembering names, either? It isn't easy for most people, BUT remembering a student's name is a powerful way to show you care.

131. DON'T be discouraged

The students who reject you in the harshest way are the students who are screaming for somebody to care for them. Unfortunately, occasional discouragement is part of a small group leader's job description.

132. DO remember how essential small groups are to the ministry

Students need to feel cared for and valued; that's why we have small groups. You are the key in that process! When students find that connection, they'll take their next steps in growing spiritually.

133. **DON'T go it alone, rookie**
Connect with other small group leaders—especially those who have been in the trenches for a few seasons. They'll be a huge help!

134. **DO ask for help when you need it**
If you come in contact with a student who is going through something that you feel you cannot handle alone, let someone else on the team know. This is the power of teamwork!

135. **DON'T give up**
This isn't going to be easy, but you are believed in and you can do it. Lean on your team. Lean on Jesus. A cord of three strands is not easily broken (Ecclesiastes 4:12). With the help of others, you can do it... and do it well!

Think about your key do's and don'ts and share them at your next small group leader meeting.

3 BENEFITS TO SPENDING TIME WITH OTHER SMALL GROUP LEADERS

Don't do small group ministry alone! Building community is one of the goals for your small group, but remember you are part of a community of other small group leaders as well. Here are some ways you can get the most out of meeting with other small group leaders in your church:

136. Share your heart

Ask God to give you a vision for your group and share that vision with others. Use what other leaders share to help strengthen your small group.

137. Share your questions and struggles

You've got great youth ministry instincts—someone believed enough in you to ask you to be part of the youth ministry team. However, you will still feel a need for direction for dealing with small group issues; share these needs with other leaders. You will find the hope you need and help for your group during that connection time. The beauty of being on a team is everybody has wisdom to offer in areas where others may be lacking. There's so much we can learn from each other... we are better together.

138. Share your successes
One of the greatest parts about being a small group team is that we can share in the joys of ministry. Did a student commit to getting baptized? Did they make a confession and expose a secret sin to find healing and forgiveness? When God is moving, share it with the team—you might be surprised at how much it means to other leaders and how it will give them hope for their group.

Make time for your regular meetings with other small group leaders. You can learn from each other and greatly improve over the course of the small group season.

This is the Lord's doing, and it is wonderful to see. This is the day the Lord has made. We will rejoice and be glad in it. Please, Lord, please save us. Please, Lord, please give us success. Bless the one who comes in the name of the Lord. We bless you from the house of the Lord. The Lord is God, shining upon us. Take the sacrifice and bind it with cords on the altar. You are my God, and I will praise you! You are my God, and I will exalt you!

(Psalm 118:23-28)

4 SIGNS YOU NEED A CO-LEADER FOR YOUR SMALL GROUP

139. Your group is too large

When a group grows, it will lose some of the special sauce that made it so attractive to students in the first place—it's small. More importantly, you'll also lose the intimacy and community that make a small group feel small. You might not need to divide the group totally; just consider adding a co-leader to help you break up the group for times of discussion and accountability.

Be careful not to abuse the co-leader by canceling when small group is not convenient for you. Keeping commitments when it's difficult honors your ministry's trust, but it also illustrates to your students the concept of sacrifice. When they know you pay a price to be there, they will value the group more. You will also retain your ability to hold them accountable when they skip out on small group next time their favorite band comes into town.

140. **You cancel too often**
It's time to get a co-leader if you cancel small group more than once every two months. Yes, people travel, schedules change, duty calls, but if it is calling too often, consider bringing in assistance to help you out. Another way to solve this problem (if you can't find a co-leader) is to partner with the leader of another group. When you are out of town, the groups can combine. When the other leader misses, you can return the favor.

141. **Your group is getting your leftovers**
Serving in a small group takes some serious effort! If your plate is too full to handle the commitment, consider adding a co-leader to give you the extra octane you haven't been able to provide. Consider asking a student's parent to join you to take some of the responsibility.

142. **You have trouble maintaining order**
You might have the right size group, but you feel overwhelmed because your students are often out of control. While there is usually a certain amount of chaos, if it isn't controlled chaos, ask for help. Remember, everyone has a rookie season before they're veterans. Don't be dejected about not being able to control your students without a little help.

140

Be honest in your assessment of needing help as a small group leader. The goal is to care for these students!

Two people are better off than one, for they can help each other succeed. If one person falls, the other can reach out and help. But someone who falls alone is in real trouble. Likewise, two people lying close together can keep each other warm. But how can one be warm alone? A person standing alone can be attacked and defeated, but two can stand back-to-back and conquer. Three are even better, for a triple-braided cord is not easily broken.

(Ecclesiastes 4:9-12)

TEND OR FEED?

There are some leaders who lean toward tending their sheep and others who feed their sheep. Understanding who you are will help you become a better leader, and identifying your weak spots tells you where you need to grow.

143. TEND: Fellowship is what you're going after. You want students to be known and cared for by an adult, mentoring relationship. Like a shepherd, you're lovingly guiding and directing your students through this wild world.

144. FEED: Discipleship is the key. Students need to be instructed in the ways of the Word and shown God's direction for their lives. While they get to nibble in the large group setting, you get the honor of giving them the prime cuts in small group (I realize sheep are vegetarians, but I love the imagery and taste of a good prime cut).

Your students get "good" from the large group time; they get "great" from the personal attention to Scripture from their small group experience. They also benefit from the opportunity to ask questions and share insights during your time together.

Tending and feeding are both important aspects of your ministry. The answer to the question "tend or feed" is "yes." I love that God entrusts us with that amazing task and that he equips us each uniquely to fulfill our roles.

IS YOUR GROUP
CLOSE OR CLOSED?

Here are some closely spelled words with vastly different results.

145. CLOSE: This word is chosen to describe a small group where incredible friendships appear. While the group is open to outsiders, there is still a history within the group of relational depth. There may be some inside jokes, but they are explained to new friends invited to participate. The bonds are strong, the culture is healthy, and there is a genuine and attractive openness that makes outsiders want to join.

146. CLOSED: These students also have incredible friendships within the group. The group is so close that no one from the outside is welcome—they even scoff at the very thought of someone joining their clique and wince at the thought of dividing the group. They have too many inside jokes, usually at the expense of outsiders, and make sure there are high expectations to be "good enough" to join their group. They sometimes project a "holier than thou" image that keeps outsiders at bay. The bonds are strong but unhealthy.

3 RULES FOR SMALL GROUP LEADERS AND SOCIAL MEDIA

We love our small group leaders to use Twitter™ and Facebook™! It seems like everyone is enjoying the benefits of social networking—so small group leaders can actually use the technology to benefit the group. However, from time to time we've had tough conversations and even had to remove small group leaders for a season of leadership because of what they put online. Apply these three simple guidelines when updating your social networks:

147. Remember your post is public

Here's the big deal—a joke that is funny between a few friends might not be funny when it's taken out of context or displayed in public view. Remember that every picture, status update, or essay becomes completely public the second you push "submit."

You can never really take it back once it's out there, so be wise and discerning with everything you post.

148. Remember your post can/will influence students

Impressionable teenagers are checking out your profile. Because they look up to you, they are eager to make a connection. Since they're always on Facebook™, they'll almost always read what you post. But it is so much more than just reading, they are seeing what you write, what you value, and what you show yourself doing. It all influences students—the good, bad, and ugly. Of course, it works the other way as well; when you use social media positively, it can have a significant influence on them, too. Unfortunately, when we slip up publicly, it can devastate or confuse students personally.

149. Remember your post is a reflection on your student ministry/church

Your character and faith are reflected in every post that you make, so if you are doubtful about something, here's a simple rule to follow: DON'T POST IT.

Just like behavior on a youth ministry trip is a reflection on the church and student ministry, know that what you post adds or detracts to the reputation of the church and ministry—and ultimately Christ.

140

If it's a questionable post ... don't do it.

My father taught me, "Take my words to heart. Follow my commands, and you will live. Get wisdom; develop good judgment. Don't forget my words or turn away from them. Don't turn your back on wisdom, for she will protect you. Love her, and she will guard you."

(Proverbs 4:4-6)

FINISHING

WELL

Thank you for your contribution to the youth ministry at your church. When you're ready to take a season off, here are some ways to leave ministry well.

143

THE APPRECIATION VACUUM

The reality of being a small group leader is that it is often a thinly rewarded, thankless job. The following statements are true for most leaders:

150. You won't get thanked very often

In the craziness of a teenager's life, the last thing they'll think about is thanking you for investing in their life. You could be making a world of difference, but more often than not, it slips their mind. When they do say thanks, it could well be several years down the road. You may find thankfulness more in their actions than their words (invitations to their games, graduation, baptism, wedding, baby dedication). But, when the thankfulness eventually arrives, it will be both memorable and meaninful.

151. You will hear more about problems than praise

Being a small group leader is a calling—if you're in it for the appreciation, you're going to quickly become disappointed. If you know that leadership is going to be a mixture of good, bad, and ugly, you'll likely last longer as a small group leader. Deal with the problems and savor the praise. I've been chastised after doing great work in students' lives by parents upset by one minor detail. The good news is if you struggle with pride, youth ministry has a way of humbling (or breaking) you into submission and reliance on God.

152. Your strength must come from your walk with God

God will give you the strength you need and endurance to finish the race. Small groups are a huge investment of your life. Make sure your leadership role is constantly supported by your growing relationship with Jesus.

140

Thank you! THANK YOU VERY, VERY MUCH. Those few words of affirmation may need to last you for a year.

As a result of your ministry, they will give glory to God. For your generosity to them and to all believers will prove that you are obedient to the Good News of Christ. And they will pray for you with deep affection because of the overflowing grace God has given to you. Thank God for this gift too wonderful for words!

(2 Corinthians 9:13-15)

4 WAYS TO RESPOND TO THE SMALL GROUP DIP

So you're more than halfway through the year, and only about half of your group is still showing up for small group... what's going on?!

153. Don't panic
Unfortunately, this is a completely normal trend. After the excitement of the school year's launch, and the momentum of a new year, things start to hit the skids during the spring season. Don't freak out if a few of your students get bogged down in school activities or begin to emphasize other priorities. It's normal, and so are you.

154. Work the phones
Make texting your friend for this season and remind your students of when and where small group is meeting. Consider planning a fun night out just to rally the troops for a relational and fun night. Start by leaving a few voicemails and asking students to remind the others in their group that they may see at school.

155. Keep parents in the loop

Parents are often aware of their student's commitment (or lack thereof) to small group—but either way make sure they're in the loop on their child's involvement. They can be a great partner in helping you fight through the dip and alerting you to any problems that may be discouraging their child from attending.

156. Finish well

Don't let low attendance distract you from being a strong leader. Stick to the basics:

• Be prepared with your lesson

• Focus on relationships

End the year strong with whoever shows up.

"The Dip"… the downward slide, right before a remarkable gain. Fight through it!

Jesus saw the huge crowd as he stepped from the boat, and he had compassion on them because they were like sheep without a shepherd.

(Mark 6:34a)

3 STEPS TO LEAVING AS A SMALL GROUP LEADER

All good things must come to an end. THANK YOU for all you've done. You've facilitated changed lives and prepared students spiritually. Way to go! Everyone understands when it's time to transition and move on to something else. When you're ready to depart youth ministry (and I hope that doesn't happen prematurely), here are a few ways you can leave right:

157. Finish your commitment

We ask each of the small group leaders to serve for a year at a time. We hope they recommit at the end of the year and come back for more, but it isn't always the case. If you sense your commitment is about to change, do your best to serve till the end of the school year if at all possible (obviously, there are always exceptions).

158. Communicate with leadership

Don't surprise the leadership by not communicating your decision to stop leading. Give ample warning so your spot can be filled before you leave. You will express love for your students in this transition by giving the primary leader time to search for a small group leader to fill your big shoes.

159. Support the ministry from afar

You know the mission and heart of the student ministry from firsthand experience and even though you're not serving anymore, cheer them on! Use your knowledge and experience to build up the perception of student ministry in your circles of influence inside and outside the church. Protect and support the student ministry in your church.

Thanks again—you will be missed!

140

You can't leave. Really, we won't let you. Ideas 157-159 were for someone else, not you.

I have fought the good fight, I have finished the race, and I have remained faithful. And now the prize awaits me—the crown of righteousness, which the Lord, the righteous Judge, will give me on the day of his return. And the prize is not just for me but for all who eagerly look forward to his appearing.

(2 Timothy 4:7-8)

3 REASONS
WHY YOUR MINISTRY TO STUDENTS MAKES A DIFFERENCE

160. You are helping teenagers grow spiritually

You are making a difference every week with your students because you are teaching and modeling the Word of God. You are loving them and helping them grow spiritually on their own, which is a gift that will last them a lifetime.

161. You are modeling Christian community

You are making a difference every minute you spend in ministry as a small group leader.

You are parenting kids with no parents. For many, their biggest impact has been as a surrogate dad for students with no father-figure. You are a mother to the motherless. You are present for the absent parent. You are making a huge difference in the lives of students as you help parent them and point them to Jesus.

Every time you call or text a teenager to check up on them, they are experiencing one of the beautiful realities within the body of Christ—a life-on-life, spiritual relationship. Every minute teaching God's Word in your small group, every minute giving a spiritual challenge over a Coke® or coffee, every minute comforting tearful students after a huge loss, you are building a caring community. All these actions are great examples of genuine fellowship.

162. You are developing your faith as you serve others

God is not just working through you to make a difference in a teenager's life, but he's also working in you to make a difference in your life. There are some spiritual truths that God will only teach us when we are serving others. We're never more like Jesus than when we serve others. The longer you're working with teenagers, the more you'll be like Jesus. Your ministry is making an eternal difference in others... and in you. Congratulations!

And all of this is a gift from God, who brought us back to himself through Christ. And God has given us this task of reconciling people to him. For God was in Christ, reconciling the world to himself, no longer counting people's sins against them. And he gave us this wonderful message of reconciliation. So we are Christ's ambassadors; God is making his appeal through us. We speak for Christ when we plead, "Come back to God!" For God made Christ, who never sinned, to be the offering for our sin, so that we could be made right with God through Christ.

(2 Corinthians 5:18-21)

ACKNOWLEDGEMENTS

From Josh:

Special thanks to the youth ministry team at Saddleback Church! You are an amazing group of volunteer small group leaders who are making a huge difference in the young lives of Southern California teenagers. It's an honor to serve alongside you.

To those who helped make this content and make it readable—you are so appreciated. Cory, thanks for the student's perspective. Dennis, thanks for taking it to the next level—you are a writing and editing machine. Katie, thanks for reading it over with your veteran heart and writing a gracious foreword. Jessica, for taking a copy of the manuscript and pretending to care about it even though I never heard back from you. Ryanne, I love your tireless heart for volunteers. Kyle, thanks for devoting hours of your life to the pages of this book, especially page 117. McGill and Fields, you are the very best of the best and I'm honored to walk with you in ministry together.

Angela, you are a wise, beautiful and loving woman. Christian, Austin, Alexis and Jadin, I love that you are the original small group in my life. Love you.

From Doug:

Thanks Josh for inviting me to help you with this project. I love you and value our friendship, and so enjoy doing ministry with you.

NOTES

NOTES

NOTES

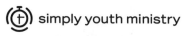

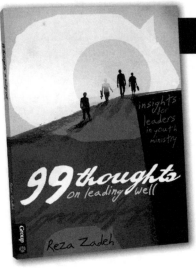